Bible Freaks & geeks

☑ S0-ARM-501

Bible Freaks & geeks

by Ed Strauss
art by Erwin Haya

Luke 2:52

ZONDERkidz

ZONDERVAN.com/
AUTHORTRACKER
follow your favorite authors

ZONDERKIDZ

Bible Freaks and Geeks
Copyright © 2007 by Edward Strauss
Illustrations © 2007 by Erwin Haya

Requests for information should be addressed to:

Zonderkidz, *Grand Rapids, Michigan 49530*

Library of Congress Cataloging-in-Publication Data

Strauss, Ed, 1953-
    Bible freaks & geeks / by Ed Strauss.
      p. cm. – (2:52)
   ISBN 978-0-310-71309-8 (softcover)
    1. Boys – Conduct of life – Juvenile literature. 2. Boys – Religious life – Juvenile literature. I.
Title. II. Title: Bible freaks and geeks.
BJ1641.S77 2007
248.8'2 – dc22   2006035695

All Scripture quotations unless otherwise noted are taken from the *Holy Bible, New International Version*®. NIV®. Copyright © 1973, 1978, 1984 by International Bible Society. Used by permission of Zondervan. All rights reserved.

Any Internet addresses (websites, blogs, etc.) and telephone numbers printed in this book are offered as a resource. They are not intended in any way to be or imply an endorsement by Zondervan, nor does Zondervan vouch for the content of these sites and numbers for the life of this book.

All rights reserved. No part of this publication may be reproduced, stored in a retrieval system, or transmitted in any form or by any means—electronic, mechanical, photocopy, recording, or any other—except for brief quotations in printed reviews, without the prior permission of the publisher.

Zonderkidz is a trademark of Zondervan.

Editor: Barbara Scott
Art direction & design: Merit Alderink

Printed in the United States of America

contents

In Bible times God's people had a slang term for *Gentiles*, which meant anybody who was not a Jew. They called them *dogs*. This is different from the modern expression, *dawg,* which means a close friend. (Example: "What's up, dawg?") Dogs back then were mean, mangy mutts gobbling gross garbage. Dogs were considered unclean, so Jews couldn't eat them or touch their dead bodies. (Like they would *want* to?)

In fact, there were a whole slew of animals they considered unclean. The book of Leviticus, chapter 11, gives the lineup: camels, coneys, rabbits, pigs, sea creatures (except fish—fish were cool), eagles, vultures, ravens, owls, storks, bats, weasels, rats, geckos, great lizards, and skinks. A skink is a lizard, by the way, not a skinny skunk.

One day God showed the apostle Peter that it was time to get over calling Gentiles unclean. Peter was up on the roof praying—the roof was flat—when he became hungry. While his meal was being prepared, he had a grossed-out vision of this large sheet being let down from heaven by its four corners. It was full of beasts, reptiles, and birds crawling all over each other. It was like a picnic gone wrong.

A voice commanded, "Get up, Peter. Kill and eat!"

Peter nearly gagged. "Surely not, Lord! I've never eaten anything [gulp] impure."

The voice said, "Do not call anything impure that God has made clean."

Peter didn't grab the nearest weasel, wring its neck with his bare hands, and force its raw body parts down his throat. He clued in that this was a vision, you know, a parable. God was saying that although the Gentiles seemed like weird critters, they were okay.

Good thing Peter got the point, 'cause a few minutes later some Gentiles knocked on the gate and invited him to the home of a Roman officer named Cornelius. When Pete got to Corny's house, he said, "You are well aware that it is against our law for a Jew to associate with a Gentile or visit him. But God has shown me that I should not call any man impure or unclean" (Acts 10:9–35). Translation: You dawgs still seem weird to me, but hey, if *God* says you're cool then you're cool.

You run into a lot of different kids in school—only instead of being called geckos, dogs, vultures, and lizards, they're called geeks, nerds, kooks, and freaks. You wouldn't normally call someone unclean these days, but you might call him seriously uncool.

Now here's the deal: if you hang with a certain group of kids, you'll be tempted to dis others who aren't part of your clique. *Don't*. To paraphrase Peter: You're well aware that a cool kid does not associate with a loser, but God has shown me that I shouldn't call anyone a loser.

No matter what kind of weird creatures other kids are—or you *think* they are—God loves them and wants you to love them. You may not mix with their crowd, you may not like what they like or wear the kind of clothes they wear, but you gotta respect them. Think that's a tough order? Read on. It gets wilder.

WHAT THIS BOOK'S ABOUT

Okay, let's talk about what this book is, and what it is not. First, it's not a dictionary of the very latest slang that came bouncin' off the radio yesterday. Some of that stuff's hot today but already old tomorrow. For example, phat is a term meaning "super cool," so when a girl calls her friend phat, she's not saying Suzy needs to seriously lay off the french fries, she's saying, "You're awesome!" But phat is already losing its popularity and may be out of use completely in two years.

Slang comes. Slang goes. Two hundred years ago during the Revolutionary War, if someone was not smart, he was called a doodle. That's why British soldiers sang the song, "Yankee Doodle," to poke fun at Americans. A hundred years ago, a stupid guy was called a dizzard. Hmmm. You don't hear that much anymore. Fifty years ago, lazy kids were called slugabeds.

Okay. That's what this book is not about. Instead, we're focusing on tried-and-proven slang names—like freak, geek, sucker, creep, and punk—and we'll show you how they describe the heroes and villains of the Bible. You might be surprised.

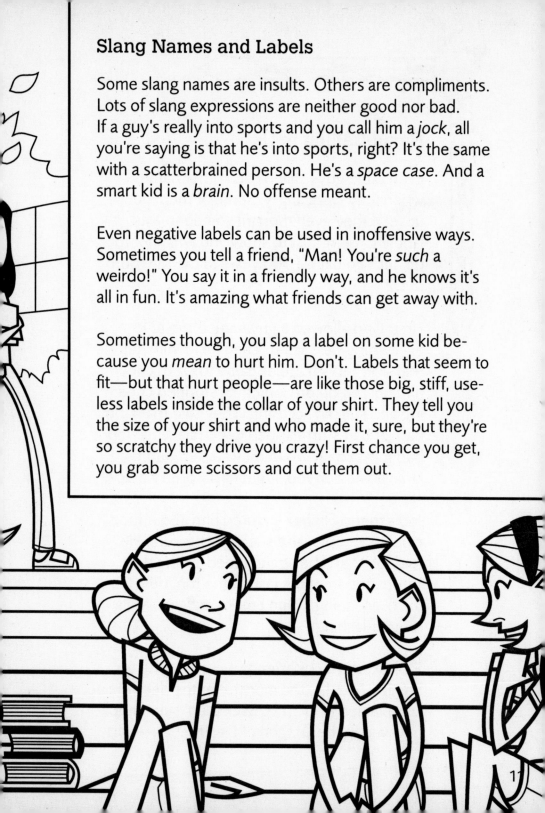

Slang Names and Labels

Some slang names are insults. Others are compliments. Lots of slang expressions are neither good nor bad. If a guy's really into sports and you call him a *jock*, all you're saying is that he's into sports, right? It's the same with a scatterbrained person. He's a *space case*. And a smart kid is a *brain*. No offense meant.

Even negative labels can be used in inoffensive ways. Sometimes you tell a friend, "Man! You're *such* a weirdo!" You say it in a friendly way, and he knows it's all in fun. It's amazing what friends can get away with.

Sometimes though, you slap a label on some kid because you *mean* to hurt him. Don't. Labels that seem to fit—but that hurt people—are like those big, stiff, useless labels inside the collar of your shirt. They tell you the size of your shirt and who made it, sure, but they're so scratchy they drive you crazy! First chance you get, you grab some scissors and cut them out.

1

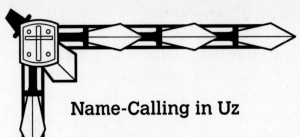

Name-Calling in Uz

Even Bible guys called each other names when they were angry. Some of them got upset if they even *thought* someone was labeling them. Just to show you what *not* to do, let's go back 3,500 years to the Kingdom of Uz.

First, God allowed a guy named Job to lose everything he owned. Then he let him get real sick. Job's buddies came to Uz to cheer him up, but before long they stopped cheering and started accusing. They said that God had let bad stuff happen to him because Job had messed up. Then they started dumping lame advice on Job. It got nasty pretty quick.

Job's friend Eliphaz lectured him about fools, clueless people, and sneaky schemers. He told Job that if he straightened up, he'd be "protected from the lash of the tongue" (Job 5:21). Meaning, "Don't make me give you a tongue-lashing!"

Job asked why his friends were ganging up on him. "Am I ... the monster of the deep?" he complained (Job 7:12). Back then, see, people believed in the Dragon of Destruction—sort of like Godzilla running loose down a city street. Bad stuff happened wherever this monster went. Job wanted to know, "Okay, bottom line, is *that* what you think I am?"

A guy named Zophar didn't say, "Yeah, you're the Godzilla-thing, dude," but he did call Job an idle talker and a mocker. He then informed him that a "witless man" could never smarten up (Job 11:1–3, 12). (Uh ... Zophar, you referring to anyone in particular?)

Job was fed up. "Come on, all of you, try again!" he snapped. "I will not find a wise man among you" (Job 17:10).

Job's bud Bildad blurted out, "Be sensible ... Why are we regarded as cattle and considered stupid in your sight?" (Can't you just see Job answering, "Look, I said you weren't wise. I did *not* call you stupid. I did not call you a cow.") Bildad began comparing people to fly maggots and said that everybody was basically a worm (Job 18:2–3; 25:6).

All this name-calling started because Job and friends were arguing about who was right—each one felt he was the smart one and the other guys were dumb—and next thing you know things got out of hand.

FUN FACT

Many English slang words come from other languages like French, German, Icelandic, and Italian. In fact, our word slang probably began as a Norwegian word. In parts of Norway, sleng means offensive language. When guys stood around calling each other names, their argument used to be called a slanging match.

Dog Names

Job and his pals weren't the only slang slingers. The Israelites had some real zingers. One day a king named Ish-Bosheth accused his top general, Abner, of being disloyal. Abner shouted back, "Am I a dog's head?" (2 Samuel 3:8). *Dog's head* meant a worthless traitor. You gotta wonder who came up with that term.

Once King David and his men were fleeing for their lives and a guy named Shimei stood by the road screaming, "Get out, get out, you man of blood, you scoundrel!" (2 Samuel 16:7). (A *scoundrel* is a lowlife.)

This ticked off David's cousin Abishai. "Why should this dead dog curse my lord the king?" he asked. "Let me go over and cut off his head" (2 Samuel 16:9). *Dead dog* was a slang expression that meant that Shimei was dead meat. Fortunately for Shimmy, David told his cousin to just keep on walking.

New Testament Slang

The Jews called Gentiles dogs, but *dog* also meant *any* dude doing bad stuff. The apostle Paul warned, "Watch out for those dogs, those men who do evil" (Philippians 3:2). You didn't want to be called a dog back then. Dogs didn't make it to heaven (Revelation 22:12–15).

Then there's a *fox*. Once some guys warned Jesus to get out of King Herod's territory. They said, "Leave this place and go somewhere else. Herod wants to kill you." Jesus replied, "Go tell that fox ... 'I must keep going'" (Luke 13:31–33). A fox is cunning, but that's not only what Jesus was getting at. Herod is not just a man of words, but of action—fox-like action.

OUTGROWING LABELS

Be careful not to brand some kid with a label like loser or imbecile just because he acts dumb now. People change. Case in point: one night the prophet Daniel had a vision of a ferocious lion with wings. Suddenly its wings were torn off—Ouch! That had to hurt!—and God stood Leo up on two feet like a man, plucked out his beast heart, and replaced it with a kind human heart (Daniel 7:2–4).

This vision wasn't about some lion angel. It was about Nebuchadnezzar, king of Babylon. Neb started off as a proud, power-hungry bully, but God humbled him and he changed into a good guy who loved God.

The point being, even bad dudes can change. If you're a Christian, you're a work in progress, meaning that God hasn't given up on you and you'll grow up. So hold out hope for other kids too.

Get Cooler

When you're mad, you're most tempted to sling slang. Maybe you don't clench your fists, turn red in the face, and start screaming insults, so you don't think you have a problem with anger. But if you call people hurtful names when they bug you, you have issues.

The solution is to ditch anger. Can it be done? Yes, it can. Proverbs 29:11 says, "A fool gives full vent to his anger, but a wise man keeps himself under control." How does a wise man do that? How can *you* keep yourself under control?

King David had a solution. He said, "I will put a muzzle on my mouth as long as the wicked are in my presence" (Psalm 39:1). What? Like a *doggie muzzle*? Yup. You got the picture—like a dog muzzle—only this is a parable. David meant that he was gonna bite his tongue. Try it next time you're tempted to call someone names.

Machos and He-men

Some guys seem to have it all. They're the top dog, the alpha male of the wolf pack, and they got game. King David was like that. He was not only handsome, but he was a wild warrior and a natural leader (1 Samuel 16:12, 18). He was macho, but he was also an all-around great guy who didn't let it go to his head. It's hard to get jealous of someone like that. You just wanna be his pal.

FUN FACT

Macho is a Spanish word that means "male." In America, macho means either (a) a top athlete, or (b) a masculine, hairy-chested wonder, or (c) some guy who's trying too hard to prove that he's (a) or (b).

Paul the Jock

A *jock* is someone who's really into sports. It can also be a slang name for a he-man wannabe, but we're talking about the real deal here.

When the apostle Paul was a kid, he went to Greek schools called *gymnasiums*. Listen, when the entire school is called a gymnasium, you just *know* they're into athletics. Paul was probably a wiry little kid who played sports and ran races like all the others. If he were around today, he'd be out kicking the soccer ball.

Years later when Paul grew up, he still talked about boxers practicing by shadowboxing and athletes training for competitions. Paul compared being a jock to living the Christian life. He said you gotta really work out and apply yourself, and stay on the track so you don't run out of bounds (1 Corinthians 9:24–27). Sounds like he'd have made a great coach!

Show-offs

Sometimes strong guys show off. But don't accuse someone of trying to be the center of attention just because they're doing something they're good at.

One day Queen Michal looked out her palace window when the priests were bringing the ark of the covenant into Jerusalem, and ... well, lookie there! If it isn't King David leaping and dancing! David was Mr. Perfect Body, and he was only dressed in a linen ephod (like a muscle T-shirt) and a loincloth. He wasn't break dancing or spinning on his head, but the man was wild.

When David came into his palace all smiling and sweaty, Michal let him have it. "How the King of Israel has distinguished himself today," she snapped, "disrobing in the sight of the slave girls!"

David replied, "It was before the Lord!" He hadn't been showing off. He was just worshiping God so wildly that he wasn't paying attention to people around him (2 Samuel 6:12–21).

There *were* glory hogs in the Bible though. In Jesus' day, whenever some religious guys went out to give money to the poor, they took a musician along. When they pulled out their money, they'd nod to the dude with the trumpet and he'd give a loud blast. Everyone in the street would jump about an inch, then turn to see Mr. Rich Religious Guy give money to a beggar (Matthew 6:2). Oh, give me a break!

Windbags

One time the mouthy king of Aram marched against Israel with a massive army. He sent a messenger to the king of Israel with a message that basically said, "I'm gonna tromp you, Little Loser Boy, until there's only handfuls of dust left! Sincerely, Ben-Hadad."

The king of Israel replied, "'One who puts on his armor should not boast like one who takes it off.'" (Translation: "You ain't even started yet, you old wind-

bag, and you think you got me beat? *Not!*") And despite Ben-Hadad's boasts, he didn't win. God helped the king of Israel pound Benny instead. (1 Kings 20:1–21.)

Hunks and Meat Chunks

A *hunk* originally meant a large chunk of meat. It still does, matter of fact. Some hunks are actually real meatheads. But as far as girls are concerned, *hunk* means a good-looking guy.

Back in ancient Israel, believe it or not, some dudes actually referred to themselves as meat chunks. They said, "This city is a cooking pot, and we are the meat" (Ezekiel 11:3). *Come again?* What they were trying to say was that they were the good stuff, the choice cuts. Everybody else was a bone.

God agreed that they were in the cooking pot, all right, but he told them they were *dead meat* and great big gobs of *scum* encrusted all over the sides of the kettle. God said he'd throw so much wood on the fire that the pot would glow red-hot and they'd be *cooked* (Ezekiel 24:3–13).

Beasts and Brutes

Today if you call someone a *beast,* you mean that he's rude or crude—like the filthy kid who runs into the house, grabs the chip bowl, and begins double-dipping. On the other hand, it could mean someone who goes all out to win. If your friend takes on a kid twice his size in a mud-wrestling competition, you'd say, "Awesome! You're a *beast,* man!"

A brute is different. If someone says, "Look at that brute!" you turn around and expect to see some guy six and a half feet tall, three hundred pounds, all hairy, and not particularly bright. This is the guy you would *not* want to mud wrestle. He would win.

They had these expressions in Bible days too. Back then, a brute was someone dumb as an animal. A poet from Crete said that people from his country were "evil brutes" (Titus 1:12). You get the impression this guy's poetry wasn't too popular back in Crete.

Goons and Bozos

Goon means a big, dumb person. A little cartoon history for you here: *goon* became popular when E.C. Segar—the cartoonist who invented Popeye—created a character called Alice the Goon. Alice had a huge body and humongous hands, so Americans started referring to big thugs as *goons*. These days *goon* means a big guy who likes to rough people up.

Another name for a guy who's all brawn and little brain is a *bozo*. A good example of a bozo is the Egyptian giant who charged into battle without plugging in his brain first. An Israelite warrior named Benaiah went one-on-one with him. All Ben had was a club, and this giant had a humongo spear. Not a fair fight, but Ben went at the big bozo, snatched the spear right out of his hand, and did him in with it (2 Samuel 23:21).

Fat and Skinny

If someone is overweight—you know, chunky—you should never call him *fatso* or *tubby*. Don't call him *phat* either and then joke, "Oh, that's just a slang word. It really means awesome." If you're his friend and you want to do him a favor, encourage him to exercise, because it's not healthy to be too heavy. But helping and hurting are two different things.

It's the same if someone's skinny. Calling him *stick man* will only make him feel bad. Think about it. *You* may be average weight, but how does it make *you* feel when a muscle-bound showoff calls you a weakling? Jesus said, "Do to others what you would have them do to you" (Matthew 7:12).

GET STRONGER

It's a good thing to be in shape. That's why the Bible says, "The glory of young men is their strength" (Proverbs 20:29). King David even talked about a champion rejoicing to run his course. The picture is of a guy who's totally jazzed about getting out on the racetrack and showing what he's got. There's nothing wrong with that. In fact, a group called Athletes in Action tells the whole world about Christians who excel in sports.

The only problem is if you get so wrapped up in your muscles that you think you're the best thing going since sliced bread. Pump iron, sure, and do your best in gym class. Just don't get pumped up with pride.

Underdog or Dawg?

If you're not part of the in-crowd—the coolest of the cool, the beautiful, the rich, and the strong—don't sweat it. *Most* of us aren't. In fact, most of the first Christians came from the poor working class. Many were slaves. Talk about bottom of the social ladder. But so what?

Paul talked about this, and if you put it in modern lingo it comes out sounding like this: "Not many of you are geniuses. Not many are powerful. Not many are cool dudes with a rep. But God chooses the dorks of the world to shame the brains. God chooses the runts to show up the machos. God chooses the kids on the bottom of the ladder and the kids everyone looks down on" (1 Corinthians 1:26–28). So if you're an underdog instead of a cool dawg, cheer up! And speaking of cheering ...

CHEERLEADERS FOR CHRIST

Originally, Jesus' disciples were called followers of the Way—meaning the Way of the Lord. Then their enemies tried to stick nasty labels on them. They accused Paul of being a ringleader of the Nazarene sect. Paul didn't like it one bit. He said, "I worship the God of our fathers as a follower of the Way, which they call a sect" (Acts 24:14).

So why aren't we still called the Way today? Where's the name Christian from? Well, "the disciples were called Christians first at Antioch" (Acts 11:26). You see, Antioch was the slang capital of the Roman Empire 'cause the pagans there liked inventing clever labels and sticking them on others.

Bible experts have studied the word Christiani (Christians), and some believe that the pagans meant it as a joke—that it was a sarcastic name meaning wild cheerleaders for Christ. At first the disciples weren't crazy about the name. They kept calling themselves the Way, but everybody else kept calling them Christians, and after a while, the name stuck.

Scum of the Earth

Anyone ever call you *scum* or *scumbag*? Scum is the slimy gook that rises to the top of the pot when you boil meat. Scum gets scooped off and dumped in the garbage. It's no fun to be called scum, but at least you're in good company. The apostle Paul said, "We have become the scum of the earth, the refuse [trash] of the world" (1 Corinthians 4:13). Paul didn't consider himself slimy garbage, but he knew that lots of people thought he was. So did he get steamed? Nah. He didn't let it bother him.

Dorks

What do kids mean if they call another kid a dork? A *dork* is not dumb. A dork is a clumsy guy who just doesn't fit in. He doesn't do cool stuff and doesn't wear cool clothes. A dork is so *uncool* that he doesn't even *know* how uncool he is.

Huh! Sounds like the Pharisees' take on John the Baptist. Back then, the Pharisees wore pretty, decorated robes and hung out with the rich crowd. But John hung out down by the Jordan River, shouted for people to repent, and dunked them in the muddy water. And talk about out-of-style clothing; this guy dressed in smelly camel's hair.

Dorky? Oh yeah. At dinner you could see John racing through the rocks chasing locusts or crawling among the canyons following wild bees back to their hives so he could snag their honey. You'd hope he got the goo off his hands before he grabbed you to baptize you! (See Mark 1:4–6.)

Freaks

The difference between a *dork* and a *freak* is that a dork wears uncool clothes but he doesn't care because he doesn't even clue in. On the other hand, a freak talks and dresses strange but he *knows* what he's doing. He just has his own look. So though the religious leaders may have written John off as a dork, he was actually a freak.

The prophet Elijah was a freak famous for unusual clothes too. Elijah once stopped some of the king's servants in the road, gave them a message, and sent them packing back to the king. Elijah didn't give his name, so when the king asked his servants to describe what the guy looked like, they replied, "He was a man with a garment of hair." Bingo! That was all that the king needed to hear. "That was *Elijah*," he said (2 Kings 1:2–8).

FUN FACT

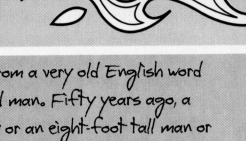

The word *freak* comes from a very old English word *freca*, which meant a bold man. Fifty years ago, a freak was a bearded lady or an eight-foot tall man or a two-headed dog. Sometimes people like that worked in a circus freak show. And if they had two heads, well, that just confirmed that they were different.

Clumsy Klutzes

If some kid stumbles with his tray and spills chicken noodle soup all over the lunchroom floor, someone's bound to say, "What a klutz!" A *klutz* is a dumb person, especially a clumsy, dumb person. It comes from the Yiddish word *klotz*, meaning a block or a lump.

The thing is, we all make mistakes, so why label someone a klutz just because he trips up? In fact, the Bible says, "Whoever gloats over disaster will not go unpunished" (Proverbs 17:5). It doesn't mean you can't laugh at some funny mistake—otherwise you could never watch *America's Funniest Home Videos* again. What it means is don't act like God just avenged you and say, "Yeah! Serves him right!"

Guess what? Even if your *enemy* stumbles, you shouldn't gloat, or the Lord will disapprove (Proverbs 24:17–18).

Spaz and Spastic

A *spaz* is a clumsy kid who makes dumb mistakes and totally loses it when he gets under pressure. Now, the fact is, some kids do overreact and do the ants-in-their-pants dance, but it's better to say they're *hyper*. Lay off calling them spastic. *Spaz* and *spastic* come from the term *spastic paraplegia*. That's an illness where someone suffers from spasms and twitching, and it's nothing to laugh about. Mock some kid with a handicap and you're mocking God his Maker (Proverbs 14:31).

Doofuses

A *doofus* is a name for a dumb, incompetent person. *Incompetent* means someone who just can't do a job right. They're just not up to it. For example, if you break half the plates while you're emptying the dishwasher, your sister might call you incompetent.

The apostle Peter was a doofus at times. He meant well, but he often made a mess of things. Like when a guy named Malchus and his soldiers came to arrest Jesus, Peter pulled out a sword, swung it, and hacked off Malchus' ear. Peter was probably aiming for his head and missed—but that's beside the point.

So now we have Malchus standing there, blood pouring down the side of his head. He's yelling with pain, and his ear is lost in the grass somewhere. Peter's standing there thinking, "Yeah ... okay ... anybody *else* want their ear cut off? Just try me."

Jesus didn't call Peter a doofus, but he *did* say, "No more of this!" Then he healed the guy's ear (Luke 22:47–51).

GET DEEPER

To *exclude* someone is the opposite of *including* them. So if you try to get in with the in-crowd, and they crowd you *out* because they figure you're not cool enough, you've just been *excluded*, dude. This often happens to Christians. When you refuse to let someone copy your homework, when you won't swear, when you don't laugh at filthy jokes, or refuse to go along with illegal stuff, some guys will call you a sissy or a dork and cut you out of their circle.

Jesus said, "Blessed are you when men hate you, when they exclude you and insult you ... because of the Son of Man" (Luke 6:22). It may not *feel* blessed at the time, especially if you think that the ultimate goal is to have a cool rep. But sometimes it's best to be excluded. It shows you're standing up for what's right.

Whatsa Nerd?

Ask some boys what a *nerd* is and they'll say it's a kid with buckteeth and thick glasses. He has few friends and wears a bow tie and pants pulled up his stomach. If you think that, you've read too many *Far Side* cartoons. To be a nerd you just have to be smart, not make friends easily, and love science or computers.

They didn't have computers back in Bible days, but when a kid named Daniel went to school in Babylon, he was so into learning and science that when King Nebuchadnezzar gave him a quiz, he found that Dan was *ten times smarter* than the "Babble-on" wise men. He made Daniel governor and put him in charge of all the wise men (Daniel 1:17–20; 2:48). Some kids like to poke fun of nerds, but hey, nerds know cool computer stuff and often get the best jobs.

Whatsa Geek?

A *geek* is another "animal." A geek is someone who's over-the-top devoted to something. Often it's computers, but it could just as well be something else—like a trekkie who's seen every episode of *Star Trek*. Think that's strange? Before your great-grandfather was born, a *geek* meant a circus performer who did strange stuff like biting the heads off live chickens.

When a guy called Uzziah was the king of Judah, he built towers on the walls around Jerusalem. He also built towers in the desert. So, um, what's with the towers? Well, Uzziah "made machines designed by skillful men for use on the towers and on the corner defenses to shoot arrows and hurl large stones" (2 Chronicles 26:9–10, 15).

These "skillful men" were weapons geeks. We're talking catapult technology—machines that hurl heavy hunks of stone at an attacking army. We're also talking honkin' big crossbows that zing armor-piercing arrows into armor-covered enemies.

Dweebs

A *dweeb* is a bookworm who's taken the whole book-reading thing so far that he hardly has a social life anymore. Some people think that a dweeb is ho-hum boring and uncool because he studies so much, but hey, a Bible guy named Ezra was your classic dweeb. He completely devoted himself to studying the law of Moses. Only thing was, nobody called Ezra names, 'cause he was a dweeb with *power*! If anyone didn't obey him, Ezra had the authority to imprison the guy, send him packing, or kill him and bulldoze his house. Not that he, um, *did* any of those things (Ezra 7:10, 25–26).

FUN FACT

Smart kids are not called eggheads because there's a little chicken inside their heads. Think of a bald mad scientist. His head looks like an egg. Also, a whiz or whiz kid is someone who is fast mentally. Whizzz is the sound you hear when something moves real fast— like an arrow whizzing past your head.

King of the Wonks

A *wonk* is like a dweeb, only even *more* into stuff that no one else finds remotely interesting. A wonk knows everything there is to know about a subject. King Solomon was not only king of Israel, but the king of wonks! Wanna know about plants? Ask Solomon. Wanna know about reptiles? Ask Solomon. Song writing? Ask Solomon. "He spoke three thousand proverbs and his songs numbered a thousand and five. He described plant life, from the cedar of Lebanon to the hyssop that grows out of walls. He also taught about animals and birds, reptiles and fish" (1 Kings 4:29–34). The guy was like a walking encyclopedia set!

GENIUSES AND EINSTEINS

You've heard of Einstein, the super genius, right? Did you know that when Einstein died, Dr. Thomas Harvey removed his brain, pickled it in formaldehyde, and kept it in a jar? He stored it behind his watercooler. Harvey wanted to study Einstein's brain to figure out why he was so smart. Guess what! Einstein's inferior parietal lobe was 15% wider than normal and the brain cells in his Sylvian fissure were packed tight together. Got that? Didn't think so. That's why Einstein was a genius and you're not.

No one pickled King Solomon's brain when he died—or if they did, we haven't found the pickle jar—but Solomon was also a lean, mean, thinking machine. "He was wiser than any other man" (1 Kings 4:31).

DOUBTING THOMAS

Some people are so skeptical that they refuse to believe something, no matter what proof you show them. After Jesus died then came back to life, the apostle Thomas refused to believe it. (That's why he was called Doubting Thomas.) The other disciples insisted they'd seen and heard Jesus, but Thomas probably asked, "Yeah, but did you touch him to be sure it wasn't just a spirit?"

They hadn't, but for sure they told Thomas about some women that had, like a lady named Mary who grabbed Jesus' feet. And Mary Magdalene held onto Jesus so tightly that he had to finally tell her to let go.

Thomas shook his head. "Unless I see the nail marks in his hands and put my finger where the nails were … I will not believe it." One week later Jesus materializes through the wall, walks straight up to Tom, and says, "Put your finger here; see my hands … stop doubting and believe." Thomas nearly had a heart attack! He was convinced! Finally! (see Matthew 28:8–9; John 20:16–29).

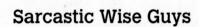

Sarcastic Wise Guys

Sarcasm is when you make cutting remarks that actually mean the opposite. Like if your baby brother chews your homework and you groan, "Isn't *this* just great!" That's sarcasm. Often sarcasm is meant to hurt, but sometimes it just helps get a point across.

For example, when Job had lost everything he owned and was sick and in pain, his friends began loading him down with dumb advice, telling him stuff he already knew. Job got so frustrated he basically told them, "Doubtless you're the only guys on earth with brains, and when you die, all knowledge will vanish from the planet" (Job 12:2). As you might've guessed, Job was being sarcastic.

GET SMARTER

Some jocks look down on smart kids. They think big muscles are better than big brains. Hey, it's great to have a six-pack, but it's better to have a packed brain—especially if the cells in your Sylvian fissure are tight-packed. Muscles will help you do more push-ups in gym class, but brains *do* win out in the long run. Like King Solomon said, wisdom can make you more powerful than the ten rulers in your city (Ecclesiastes 7:19).

On the other hand, if you're smart, don't be the wise guy who shows off knowledge and uses it to put other people down. No one appreciates a know-it-all. Knowledge that's used to dis others is not real wisdom. "'Let not the wise man boast of his wisdom'" (Jeremiah 9:23). If you're smart, be humble about it.

Slackers

Jesus told a story about a farmer with two slacker sons. Now, a *slacker* is someone who tries to get out of doing work or else does a slow, sloppy job when he does do it. Know anyone like that? When it comes time to clean up the toys, you're putting them all back in the box while (fill in name) keeps playing? Or maybe it's *your* name in the blank.

Anyway, this father said to Son One, "Son, go and work today in the vineyard." Son One was not only a slacker, he also had an attitude, 'cause he answered, "No." Later his conscience got the better of him and he went. He did a *good job* too—which shows that even slackers can change.

Meanwhile, Dad didn't know that Son One had changed his mind, so he told Son Two to go work in the vineyard. This guy turned out to be the *real* slacker. He said sure, no sweat, he'd go. "No sweat" was right. This slacker was a non-sweating no-show. No telling where he goofed off to, but it wasn't Grape City (Matthew 21:28–31).

A sluggard or slug is someone who's slow-moving or lazy. When people saw a slimy little animal like a snail without a shell crawling along soooo slow, they said, "What a slug!" And that's how slugs got their name. The Bible also talks about slothful people—also called sloths. A sloth is a very lazy person who barely moves. When explorers in South America saw hairy critters hanging in the tree branches, moving about an inch a year, they said, "Whoa! What a sloth!" And the name stuck.

Slugs and Sloths

The Bible talks a lot about *sluggards*, so even though that slang's a bit old, you need to know that it means a lazy person. Otherwise you could be reading the Bible one day, see what it says about sluggards, and think, "Man! *That* dude's in bad shape!" and not realize that it's talking about *you*. (Just kidding.)

King Solomon described a farmer who was so lazy that his vineyard grew over with thorns and weeds. But did he weed it? Nah. Couldn't be bothered. His stone wall fell down and pigs got in and gobbled his grapes. But will he fix it? Some day. His roof leaked. But did he get up out of bed and repair it? Nope. He just rolled over and went back to sleep (Proverbs 24:30–34; 26:14; Ecclesiastes 10:18).

All this is bad enough, but here's the kind of sluggard you don't want over for dinner. Back in Israelite times they didn't have plates, forks, or spoons. When a family ate, everybody stuck their fingers in one big dish and grabbed food. That's already rough if you're not used to it. But Solomon talked about the ultimate lazy guy: "The sluggard buries his hand in the dish; he is too lazy to bring it back to his mouth" (Proverbs 26:15). So he just *sits* there, half asleep, his hairy paw *buried* in the food bowl. (Still hungry?)

Slouches and Couch Potatoes

A *slouch* is a lazy, inactive person, someone who lies around doing nothing—in other words, a *couch potato*. Or is that a *slouch potato*? God got really upset at some lazy Israelite slouches that lay around on couches and beds drinking wine and strumming on harps while their country went to the dogs. God got so upset that he compared the couch potatoes of Bashan to cows! So would they be *couch cows*? (see Amos 4:1; 6:1–7.)

Slobs and Slummin' It

A *slob* is someone who doesn't bother to dress in clean clothes, comb his hair, or bathe. That's fine if you're in a war. You don't shampoo when someone's shooting at you. You don't take a shower if someone just blew your bathroom away with a bazooka. When Nehemiah was building the walls around Jerusalem, and enemies threatened to attack, his crew had to be ready to wake up fighting in the middle of the night. They didn't change their clothes for weeks (Nehemiah 4:23)!

But here's the catch: if you're not dodging bullets, there's *no* excuse for being a slob. The Bible says, "Bathe with water" (Leviticus 15:11). By the way, *slob* comes from the Irish word *slab* which means "mud."

Moochers and Leeches

A *moocher* is a kid who's always there with his hand out when you buy a snack at the store. He'll chew your gum, chomp on your chips, and slurp your brain freeze. Moochers are always bumming stuff off others. They wear out the welcome rug real quick.

A *leech* is a little critter the size of a slug with a huge mouth. It attaches itself to you and sucks your blood. A leech is always saying, "Give! Give!" (Proverbs 30:15). No surprise that a mooch is often called a leech.

Before King David was king, he and his men were living in the wilderness near the land of a sheep rancher named Nabal. All summer, David and his warriors helped guard Nabal's shepherds and sheep. When it came time to shear (cut) the wool off the sheep, David sent some men, saying that since it was party time and all, could Nabal spare some food?

Nabal thought David was mooching. He snarled, "Why should I take my bread and water and the meat I have slaughtered for my shearers, and give it to men coming from who knows where?" Not smart. Fortunately, Nabal's wife loaded a dozen donkeys with snacks and trucked them out to David (1 Samuel 25:1–19). The moral? Be wary of moochers but hey, share with guys who deserve it!

Pigs and Gluttons

It's one thing if a bunch of hungry guys come in, wolf down food, gulp down hot dogs, and vacuum out the fridge. They're not gluttons. They're just hungry dudes. A *glutton* is the kid who gets to the lunch table early and inhales the entire pizza, leaving nothing for others. Gluttons are also called pigs and hogs. The Bible says, "Do not join those who ... gorge themselves on meat, for drunkards and gluttons become poor" (Proverbs 23:20–21).

Of course, Jesus' enemies accused him of being a glutton simply because he enjoyed a good meal and didn't skip food all the time (Matthew 11:19). So don't be quick to label some kid a glutton. He might just be a growing boy.

Pack Rats

Jesus told a story about a stingy pack rat who had tons of goodies but refused to share with others. This rich guy had such a good crop one year that his barns weren't big enough to hold all the grain. Instead of sharing with the poor, he decided to tear down his barns, build bigger ones, and hoard it all. God said, "You fool! This very night your life will be demanded from you. Then who will get what you have prepared for yourself?" Good question.

That's why Jesus warned, "Be on your guard against all kinds of greed; a man's life does not consist in the abundance of his possessions." (See Luke 12:15–21.) Life is more than hoarding piles of toys or playing all day with them.

Get Cooler

If some kid lies around all day playing video games and never lifts a finger to help around the house, that's not right. If he doesn't even clean his own room, you *know* there's something wrong with this picture.

Some boys are happy to let their parents pick up after them. They're not concerned that this makes life harder for others. Hmmm ... sounds like some guys Jesus talked about. They pile heavy loads on others "but they themselves are not willing to lift a finger to move them" (Matthew 23:4).

Don't let that be you. Help your poor mom out. If you wanna grow up into a man of God, a good place to start is taking responsibility for your clothes and your room now.

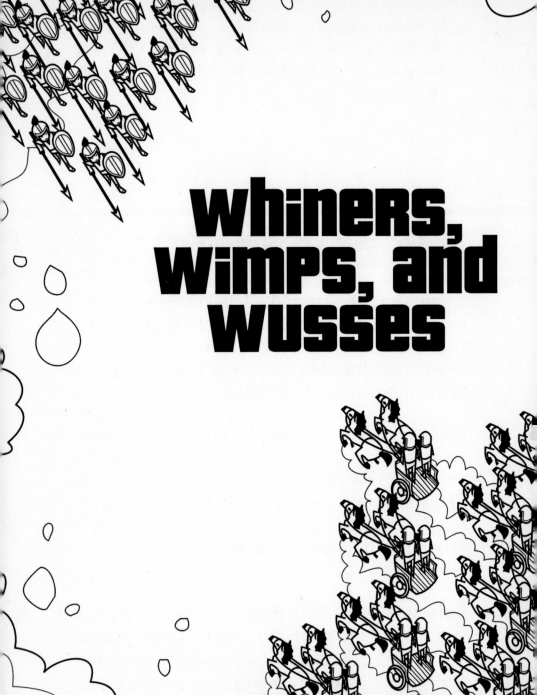

whiners, Wimps, and WUSSES

Cowards and Wusses

Kids call someone a *coward* if they're scared of doing something. But you're *not* a coward if you're headed into battle (or the dentist's office) and you're scared.

One day the Philistines invaded Israel with 3,000 chariots and zillions of soldiers carrying zillions of swords. King Saul had zero chariots, 600 men, and only (gulp!) two swords. Most Israelites wussed out. They either hid in the bushes or took off running. But "Saul remained at Gilgal, and all the troops with him were quaking with fear." His men were so scared they were shaking like Jell-O, but they stood their ground. They were no cowards (1 Samuel 13:5–7, 22).

FUN FACT

Coward comes from the Latin word *cauda*, which means "tail." Get the picture? A coward is someone who runs away with his tail between his legs. Wuss means "coward," but where did the word wuss come from? No one really knows. Someone just invented it one day.

Whiners and Complainers

When the Israelites were slaves in Egypt, they worked from sunrise to sunset, and guys with whips laid lashes on their backs. Then God took the Israelites out of Egypt. Food was a bit scarce out in the desert so they complained, "If only we had died ... in Egypt! There we sat around pots of meat and ate all the food we wanted!"

Hey! You need food? Just *say* so! God then miraculously supplied stuff called manna that tasted as sweet as honey. It was so delicious that the Bible called it angels' food, bread from heaven (Exodus 16:1–15, 31).

Were the Israelites content? Nah. After a while they whined, "Now we have lost our appetite; we never see anything but this manna!" (Numbers 11:4–6). Man!

Their complaining was ridiculous. But you know, kids today do it all the time and it sounds just as bad.

Chickens

A lot of people think the apostle Peter was a chicken when he denied that he knew Jesus. First Peter insisted, "Even if I have to die with you, I will never disown you." After a mob arrested Jesus, Peter followed them to the high priest's house. That's where he got cornered. Three times people accused him of being Jesus' disciple, and three times Peter denied it. When the rooster crowed, Peter realized what a chicken *he* had been (Mark 14:31, 66–72).

After Peter repented, he made up his mind that he would never deny Jesus again. And he didn't. Church history says he walked straight into Rome during a very dangerous time and was crucified.

Wimps

A *wimp* is a guy who whimpers over the littlest thing. When Paul and Barnabas headed out to preach the gospel in new cities, they took a young guy named Mark. Now, Mark did fine for the first while, but when the going got tough, he wimped out and headed home to his mommy in Jerusalem. Paul got so upset that he refused to *ever* take Mark on a trip again (Acts 13:4–5, 13; 15:36–40).

Fortunately, Mark grew up and became such a top-notch worker that he became the pick of the season, and Paul called him to join his team (2 Timothy 4:11). Mark even wrote the gospel of Mark. So don't write a kid off as a permanent pushover if he wimps out once. Chances are he'll make it up later.

Weaklings

When a kid can't keep others from snatching the basketball away or he's wiped after ten laps around the gym, a lot of boys groan, "Pathetic!" or "Weakling!" Okay. Some kids just aren't as strong as the rest, but why get on their case for that?

In the Bible, when God ordered Gideon to lead the troops into battle, Gideon said, "How can I save Israel? My clan is the weakest in Manasseh, and I am the least in my family" (Judges 6:15). Gideon said he was the weakest of the weak, but God was the one who was going to win the battle anyway, so he wasn't looking for a strong guy. All he needed was a man with enough faith to obey him—and Gideon was that man.

Doormats

You wipe your shoes on doormats before going in the house—or you should—so people who get stepped on are called *doormats*. Some Christians think they *should* let people walk all over them. Well, it's wise to ignore insults, but there are times when you gotta stand up for your rights.

One day in Jerusalem, some Roman soldiers arrested Paul because they thought he was a troublemaker. They were coming out of the back room with killer whips, getting ready to beat the living tar out of him, when Paul demanded, "Is it legal for you to flog a Roman citizen who hasn't even been found guilty?" The officer freaked. Oh yeaaah. He could get in *huge* trouble for beating a Roman citizen (Acts 22:24–29).

As a citizen of your country, you have rights. Now, don't go to the opposite extreme and accuse someone of harassment if they only tease you, but there *are* laws in place to protect you from being hurt.

FICKLE, FAIR-WEATHER FRIENDS

Once, Paul and Barnabas went preaching the gospel in a city called Lystra where they met a crippled guy. Paul prayed for him to be healed, and instantly the man leaped up and began walking. The crowds went wild. "The gods have come down to us in human form!" they whooped. They decided Paul must be the fast-talking Greek god Hermes (Mercury), and Big Barnabas was the big god guy, Zeus. The Lystrans dragged bulls to the city gate to sacrifice to them, and our guys barely persuaded them that they were not gods.

A fickle person is someone who changes his or her mind easily. To show how fickle this crowd was, a short while later some enemies showed up in the city and persuaded the Lystrans that Paul and Barnabas were criminals. A day earlier, the Lystrans had been on their knees worshiping Paul and Zeus ... er ... I mean, Barnabas. Now they picked up rocks, used Paul for target practice, and then dumped him outside the city gate thinking he was dead. Now is that fickle or what? (See Acts 14:8–20.)

Get Deeper

When God told the Israelites to conquer the land of Canaan, the Israelites gave five big excuses why they couldn't do it:

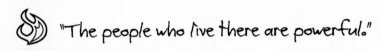 "The people who live there are powerful."

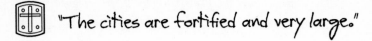 "The cities are fortified and very large."

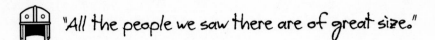 "The land we explored devours those living in it."

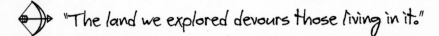 "All the people we saw there are of great size."

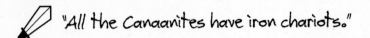 "All the Canaanites have iron chariots."

So what? As Caleb and Joshua argued, "We should go up and take possession of the land, for we can certainly do it ... The Lord is with us!" (See Numbers 13:27–14:9; Joshua 17:16.) You can be weak, afraid, and all the rest, but if you trust in God despite that, you can do great things. Your problems won't just vanish, but God will help you take care of them.

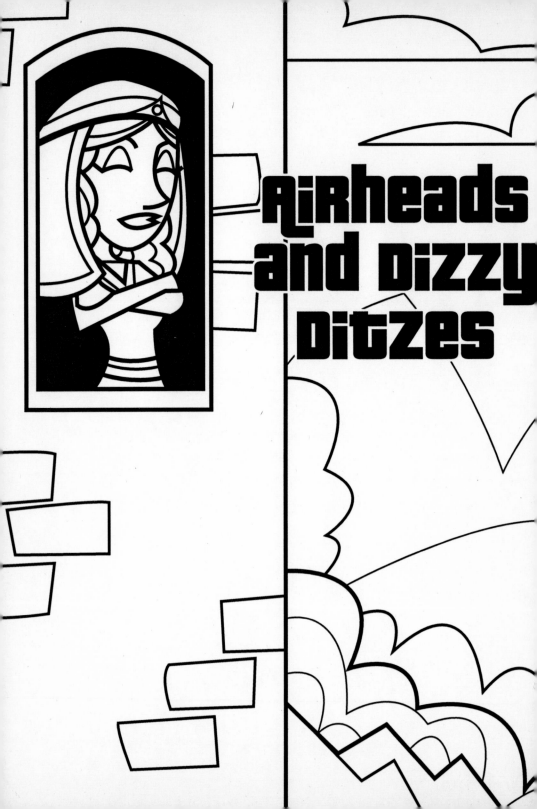

Airheads and Bimbos

Airheads are people who are totally clueless and shallow, like their heads are full of air instead of brains. And while we're talking about airheads, we might as well talk about Jezebel. She was such a wicked queen that God ordered a general named Jehu to wipe her out. Now Jezebel *knew* that Jehu was coming to execute her, so what does she do? Order her guards to fight? Try to escape? No, not this bimbo!

"When Jezebel heard about it, she painted her eyes, arranged her hair and looked out a window" (2 Kings 9:30). *Helllooo?*

Worse yet, when Jehu came roaring in the gate on his chariot, Jezzy leaned out the window and began trash-talking him. *Earth calling Jezebel!* Yeah, earth calling, all right. Some servants pushed her out the window, she hit the earth, and that was that.

Legally Blonde Jerusalem Girls

Ever seen pretty girls who *know* they're pretty? They're all gaga over their hair and clothes and bling-bling. They walk with delicate steps and get all flirty and giggly when good-looking guys walk by.

God had their number back in Bible times. Isaiah said, "The women of Zion are haughty, walking along with outstretched necks, flirting with their eyes, tripping along with mincing steps, with ornaments jingling on their ankles" (Isaiah 3:16). God warned that if they didn't repent, he would snatch away their headbands, necklaces, perfume bottles, nose rings, fine robes, purses, and mirrors.

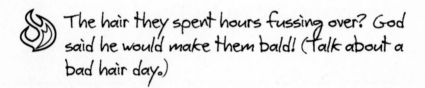 The hair they spent hours fussing over? God said he would make them bald! (Talk about a bad hair day.)

Snatching away their nose rings? Ouch! You know that had to hurt!

Snatching their purses? Does that make God a purse snatcher? Okay, okay. No, it doesn't. But the point is, God did some serious stuff to get people's attention (Isaiah 3:17–23).

Egotistical Dudes

Remember Prince Charming in the movie *Shrek 2*? He was a self-centered guy in love with his own looks. Prince Absalom in the Bible was like that. "In all Israel there was not a man so highly praised for his handsome appearance as Absalom." Abby was so proud of his hair that he grew it butt-long and only cut it when it became too heavy. Before trim time, he'd first weigh his lovely locks, and his hairdo weighed nearly *five pounds*!

Funny thing was, when Abby led a battle against King David, his hair was his downfall. Absalom's long, lovely locks got tangled up in an oak tree, and that was the end of him (2 Samuel 14:25–26; 18:9).

HISTORY OF DUDES

Nowadays, every kid calls every other kid dude. A dude is a friend, someone who's cool. Back in your great-grandma's day, dude meant a fool who followed the latest fashions. A dude was also called a fop, a vain guy who tried to get people to admire his clothes. Jesus rebuked the Pharisee fops who loved long robes with big, colorful tassels. "Everything they do is done for men to see" (Matthew 23:5).

Another name for a dude back then was a coxcomb. That comes from those wobbly red thingies on top of a rooster's head—the cock's comb. A coxcomb meant a showoff strutting around like a rooster, trying to get people to think he was hot stuff. King Solomon said strutting roosters were cool (Proverbs 30:29-31), but he meant the real deal, not rooster wannabes.

So, what's up, dude?

Snobs

A *snob* is someone who sticks his nose up in the air to ignore you. That's why snobs are called *stuck-up*. We're talking snot cannons aimed at the sky. There were snobs in the Bible too—religious snobs. The Bible calls them "holier-than-thou." This comes from Isaiah 65:5 (KJV), where religious people shouted at others, "Come not near to me; for I am holier than thou." *Riiight*.

FUN FACT

A person who makes snitty comments in a mocking tone of voice used to be called a snit. Snit is related to snot. It comes from the Scandinavian word snite, which means to wipe or blow the nose. So a snit is something like a booger.

Rhoda the Ditz

A *ditz* is a person who acts dizzy or scatterbrained. Of course, even smart people have ditzy moments—like Rhoda. The story goes like this: Peter had been arrested by King Herod and was in prison, so lots of Christians gathered in a house to pray for him. Answered prayer! God sent an angel to bust Peter out of prison, and one happy Pete dashed down the street and showed up at the house in the middle of the night.

When Peter knocked on the outer gate, a servant girl named Rhoda went to answer. When she recognized Peter's voice, Little Miss Space Case was so giddy that she forgot to open the gate. She ran back into the house squealing, "Peter is at the door!"

The Christians told Rhoda, "You're out of your mind!"

Meanwhile, Pete's out there in the street, hoping no Roman patrol sees him. He doesn't wanna be Roman roadkill, so he keeps knocking. And knocking. When the Christians finally opened the door and saw Peter, they were astonished (Acts 12:1–16).

They probably apologized to Rhoda: "Sorry for saying you lost your mind." And Rhoda probably told Peter, "Sorry for being such a ditz." Okay, everyone! Group hug!

Talkers and Gossips

Some people are real talkers—no problem there. But when kids keep on talking when they have nothing to say, you know things are gonna get out of control. Some Bible thoughts on that:

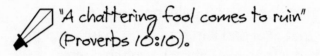
"A chattering fool comes to ruin" (Proverbs 10:10).

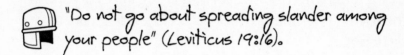
"Do not go about spreading slander among your people" (Leviticus 19:16).

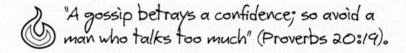
"A gossip betrays a confidence; so avoid a man who talks too much" (Proverbs 20:19).

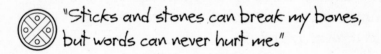
"Sticks and stones can break my bones, but words can never hurt me."

Wait! That last one wasn't a Bible verse, and it's *not true!* Words can hurt big time. King David said that some people "sharpen their tongues like swords and aim their words like deadly arrows" (Psalm 64:3). This is symbolic. You got that, right? King David was not talking about the X-Men. He was talking about people who said hurtful things.

Tattletales and Snitches

When David was running away from insane King Saul, he stopped briefly in Nob, where the priest Ahimelech lived. Ahim was a cool guy. He shared his food with David and his men, and since they had no weapons, he gave Dave a sword. David said thanks and moved on out.

What Ahim had done was totally innocent, since he didn't know that Saul had it in for David. Saul wouldn't have found out either, except that a snitch named Doeg told him. Result? Saul had Doeg kill everyone in the town (1 Samuel 21:1–9; 22:9–19). Doeg was one dirty dog.

Of course, you gotta report *bad* stuff—like if some little kid's getting bullied. So what if the bully calls you a snitch or an informer? You gotta break the code of silence and do what's right. "Speak up for those who cannot speak for themselves ... defend the rights of the poor" (Proverbs 31:8–9).

Suck-ups and Flatterers

Doesn't it bug you when someone spreads on cheesy compliments an inch thick—especially if they're only buttering you up 'cause they want you to do them a favor? Well, once there was a lawyer named Tertullus who wanted Governor Felix to do him a favor: kill the apostle Paul.

So listen as Tert begins sucking up to the governor—all of it pure baloney. He said, "We have enjoyed a long period of peace under you, and your foresight has brought about reforms in this nation. Everywhere and in every way, most excellent Felix, we acknowledge this with profound gratitude."

Just when Felix is about to say, "Hey! Stop spreading it on so thick!" Tertullus says, "But in order not to weary you further, I would request that you be kind enough to hear us briefly" (Acts 24:1–4).

Felix probably thought, "Okaaay, just don't give me that 'everywhere and in every way' stuff again."

Chumps and Suckers

A *chump* is someone who's not only ignorant, but easily fooled—in other words, a sucker. Well, there were two hundred party-loving officials in King David's day, and when Absalom went to Hebron, he told them he was going to "worship the Lord," and he invited them along. Of course, there'd be a banquet to follow, and who didn't love a party?

The officials didn't ask a lot of questions. Off they went to Hebron. Not long after they got there, trumpets started blowing and Absolom's servants shouted, "Absalom is king!" ("Oh man! I can't believe I fell for the old 'come-to-the-party' trick!") The two hundred chumps suddenly realized that they were chumps (2 Samuel 15:1–11). The lesson here: Don't be a chump. Ask questions.

Hypocrites

Before Jesus' day, it was cool to be a hypocrite. The Greek word *hypocrite* means to play a part—in other words, be an actor. Many Romans and wealthy Jews loved to go to the theaters and watch the latest play, so hypocrites were celebrities. When Jesus called the Scribes and Pharisees hypocrites, he was saying they were pretending to be godly, but they didn't practice what they preached (Matthew 23). Since then, it isn't cool to be a hypocrite anymore.

GET STRONGER

The Bible says that Rachel was "lovely in form, and beautiful" and Absalom was "praised for his handsome appearance" (Genesis 29:17; 2 Samuel 14:25). Well, *good for them!* But what did the hundreds of other Hebrew heroes look like—Samson, Joshua, Jonah, Ruth, and Esther? We have no idea, and it really doesn't matter.

When the prophet Samuel was out shopping for a king, God told him to go check out Jesse's sons. The first son that strolled past was Eliab. Samuel thought, "Oh yeah, this guy's the king!"

God said, "Do not consider his appearance or his height … Man looks at the outward appearance, but the Lord looks at the heart" (1 Samuel 16:1–7). Sure enough, God picked the youngest son, David. Not that David was bad looking, but the point is, God keeps tabs on what's in your heart. It was true then, and it's true now.

Dumb Dummies

Being *dumb* didn't used to mean stupid. When the King James Version of the Bible talks about Jesus healing *dumb* people (Matthew 9:32–33), it means people who can't speak. Mute, in other words. When Zacharias talked back to Gabriel, the angel took Zacharias' voice away. He told Zach, "Thou shalt be dumb" (Luke 1:20 KJV). Gabriel was not saying, "Please be stupid." He was saying, "Nuff sassin' back from you."

It didn't take long for *dumb* to go from meaning someone who couldn't talk to meaning someone who stood there with their mouth hanging open because they were clueless. That's today's meaning of *dumb*.

A mannequin in a store window is called a *dummy* because it can't speak, not because it's stupid. (It's beyond stupid. It has *no* brains whatsoever.)

Dolts and Dull Dudes

A *dolt* is a heavy, unintelligent fellow, and dolt comes from the word *dull*. Not *dull* as in boring. Think of a dull pencil that desperately needs to be sharpened. Some people aren't very sharp either.

Eglon was the very fat and not-so-bright king of Moab, and he was a dolt. He defeated Israel, and then ruled it with a heavy hand and made them pay heavy taxes. (Everything about this guy was heavy.) Now, an Israelite named Ehud had had enough, so when he went to pay taxes, he hid a sword under his robe. Eglon never bothered to have his guards frisk Ehud. Dolt decision one.

After giving Eglon the tax money, Ehud said, "I have a secret message for you, O king!" Eglon sent his armed guards out of the

room. Dolt decision two. Suddenly Ehud whipped out his sword out and stabbed Eglon. Eggy was so fat that the entire sword—blade and handle—disappeared into his belly (Judges 3:12–22). Eglon may have been dull, but Ehud's blade certainly was not.

Dodos

Dodos were fat birds about the size of a turkey. One day, ships full of hungry people showed up at Dodo Island with clubs. They walked up and began beaning the birds. Dodos couldn't fly, but they didn't even *try* to break away. They just stood there glassy-eyed as the dodos next to them got hit. Bonk. Bonk. Bonk. Next thing you know, the last dumb dodo was dead. Ever since then, people who stand around not cluing in have been called *dodos*.

King Solomon said that a wise man sees danger coming and gets out of the way, but clueless guys don't clue in and suffer big-time (Proverbs 22:3).

Stupid and Dazed

It's not cool to go around calling people stupid, but the fact is, some people *are* stupid. King Solomon said, "He who hates correction is stupid" (Proverbs 12:1). So, um, if your mom corrects you and you get all steamed and worked up about it, you just entered the Stupid Zone.

These days *stupid* means "dumb," but guess what? Stupid comes from a Latin word *stupere* which meant *dazed*—like if a guy gets hit in the head and stands there stunned. So *stupid* doesn't just mean low IQ. It could mean someone who's normally with it, but is just stupefied for the moment. Like if you tell a joke and your buddy doesn't get it.

Zombies

Zombie is an African word for a corpse that walks around—in other words, the living dead. These days *zombie* often doesn't have such a strong meaning. If you say, "Freddy looks like a zombie," you mean he's either dead tired, walking around in a daze, or just isn't thinking straight.

A couple times in the Bible, God raised corpses back to life and they walked around wrapped up in grave bandages—scaring people out of their wits! (See 2 Kings 13:20–21; John 11:38–44.) Of course, these guys weren't zombies because they were walking dead. They were alive again!

Idiots and Imbeciles

At one time, almost everyone in the world was an idiot. Why? The Greek word *idiōtēs* means a private citizen, an ordinary Joe with no special education. Back then, you could begin a speech saying, "My fellow idiots ..." and no one would be offended.

These days, *idiot* means someone who's *very* dumb. Some kids overuse the word, but truth be told, some people *do* idiotic things. Esau, for example: this big, hairy brute got hungry one day and traded his birthright—thousands of sheep, goats, cattle, camels, and tents full of gold and silver—for a bowl of beans (Genesis 25:29–34). By the time Esau was done, about all he had left was gas. (Well, not quite, but you get the picture.)

Imbecile used to mean weak. So English poets like Barrow used to write pretty poems saying how we are all imbeciles without God. (Uh ... *okaaay.*) These days when people say imbecile, they mean weak-*minded.* That could be why Barrow's poems aren't so popular anymore.

Dunces

Hundreds of years ago there was a Catholic priest
named John Duns Scotus from Duns, Scotland. John
was so brilliant that when other smart guys argued with
him, John just shredded them. John's followers were
called *Dunsmen* and *Dunces*. John was *so* smart that it
made his opponents look dumb, so to make themselves
feel better they said *he* was the dumb one. Then it
wasn't cool to be a *Dunce* anymore.

Years ago in America, if a student wasn't very bright,
the teacher sat him on a stool in the corner and stuffed
on his head a cone-shaped paper hat, called a *dunce
cap*. It wasn't a thinking cap. It didn't make the kid any
smarter.

In 1993, Pope John Paul II decided that people had
made fun of John Duns long enough, so he declared
that the Scot was a saint.

FUN FACTS

A clown is someone who acts silly to get everyone laughing. Clown comes from the Icelandic word klunni, which means a clumsy, ignorant fellow. Long ago, clowns also used to be called fools, because they did foolish things to make people laugh. They were also called jokers, jesters, and buffoons. These days, when one of your pals is trying too hard to be funny and starts telling lame, corny jokes, he's called a cornball.

Morons

Some names have such negative meanings that you shouldn't use them. Example: back in Jesus' day, if you were super mad at someone, you called them *moros*, which means "moron." Only Jesus said not to do it! He warned that anyone who called his brother "raca" (empty-head, brainless) had to answer to the top priests, but anyone who said, "fool" (moron) was in danger of the fire of hell (Matthew 5:22).

You may wonder why, if the word *moron* was so bad, did Jesus say to the Scribes and Pharisees, "You blind fools [morons]!" (Matthew 23:17). Well, that's what those hypocritical religious leaders *were*. Jesus was stating a fact. His irons were hot but he was branding the right cows.

But for you to call your brother a moron when you know he's *not*—he just goofed up—that's slapping the wrong label on him. It's accusing him falsely, and the Bible says, "You shall not give false testimony against your neighbor" (Exodus 20:16).

Got that? Jesus can judge people because he's God and judges justly. But we're mere mortals, and it's not our place to accuse people of being morons—or retards or losers. It's best to just cut those words from your vocabulary.

Witty Words

Wit means the power to think, so someone who has a quick sense of humor is called a *wit* or *witty*. On the other hand, *witless* doesn't mean someone who isn't funny. It means "without sense." Incidentally, you can be driven out of your wits and even be driven to your wit's end, but you can't walk there. In closing this witty subject, here are some final wit words: nitwit, halfwit, dimwit, dull-witted, slow-witted, and thick-witted.

PROVERBS ABOUT FOOLS

Everyone gets a little foolish at times, but here are some warning signs from the Bible that let you know if you're starting to act like a genuine, certifiable fool:

THE WAY A FOOL THINKS:

"The way of a fool seems right to him, but a wise man listens to advice" (Proverbs 12:15).

THE WAY A FOOL SPEAKS:

"The mouth of the fool gushes folly" (Proverbs 15:2).

"Every fool is quick to quarrel" (Proverbs 20:3).

"A fool ... delights in airing his own opinions" (Proverbs 18:2).

"The fool rages and scoffs, and there is no peace" (Proverbs 29:9).

THE WAY A FOOL ACTS:

"A fool is hotheaded and reckless" (Proverbs 14:16).

"As a dog returns to its vomit, so a fool repeats his folly" (Proverbs 26:11).

RESULTS OF BEING A FOOL:

"A chattering fool comes to ruin" (Proverbs 10:8).

"Folly brings punishment to fools" (Proverbs 16:22).

EVERYONE ELSE CAN SEE IT:

"The fool lacks sense and shows everyone how stupid he is" (Ecclesiastes 10:3).

"Their folly will be clear to everyone" (2 Timothy 3:9).

GET SMARTER

If you feel a bit dumb or ignorant, don't sweat it. The apostle Paul said, "When I was a child, I talked like a child, I thought like a child, I reasoned like a child" (1 Corinthians 13:11). Paul wasn't putting little kids down. He was simply saying that they don't know as much as adults.

But you don't have to wait till you're fully grown to be smarter and crunch facts faster. If you go to school you can get smarter day after day. Just apply yourself and learn. Sometimes you might wish you could be like a computer: put on a helmet, press a button, and get a massive download, but life's not like that. It takes time to learn. It takes keepin' at it. So keep at it.

David the Madman

The word *mad* means crazy, so a *madman* means a crazy man. Well, one day David went to the city of Gath. Some Philistines recognized him as the guy who had killed Goliath, so they dragged him to their king, Achish. David was desperate to get away, so he clawed on the door like a doggie and let drool slobber down his beard.

Achish growled, "He is insane! ... Am I so short of madmen that you have to bring this fellow here to carry on like this in front of me?" (1 Samuel 21:10–15). The guards showed David the door and he staggered off, probably blowing spit bubbles and muttering to himself. Soon as he was out of sight though, David straightened up and made a run for it.

Cracked and Crazy

These days *crazy* can mean something unexpected—a surprise that's cool or great. ("Hey, dude! I got a skateboard for my birthday!" "Crazy, man!") But of course, *crazy* is most famous for meaning insane. The word has some history to it: *craze* comes from the old English word *crasen*, which means cracked or broken.

It used to be when an elevator wasn't working, the people stuck inside it would say, "Oh, bother! The elevator's crazy again!" After a while, if some guy's mind wasn't working, they said the *person* was crazy.

That's also why if someone isn't thinking straight, people say he's *cracked*. Another thing, when machinery wasn't working, people said that there must be some *loose wires* or a *screw loose*. Soon they were saying that about people too.

Maniacs and More Madmen

Remember General Jehu? He was the guy who killed King Joram and his idol-worshiping witch-queen, Jezebel. We've already talked about Jezebel, but there's something you should know about Jehu too.

When Jehu took off in his chariot for the palace, King Joram saw this cloud of dust in the distance and asked who was coming. (Back then they didn't have cell phones or binoculars.) The lookout couldn't quite make out the driver but he could see that the chariot was burning dirt faster than chariots were made to travel, so he said, "The driving is like that of Jehu son of Nimshi—he drives like a madman" (2 Kings 9:20).

Madman alrighty! Jehu was not only Mr. Road Rage, but he was wild in everything he did. He was so high energy that he single-handedly wiped out all the priests of Baal in the nation. Jehu was God's man, but don't get the idea that he was a nice guy. He was a maniac! Have you seen *The Chronicles of Narnia: The Lion, the Witch, and the Wardrobe*? Jehu was as fierce as Oreius the centaur (half-man, half-horse) who fought the White Witch.

Wackos and Whacked

The word *wacko* or *wacky* comes from the word *whack*. You get the picture: some guy gets bonked in the head and starts acting bonkers. Lots of kids do

wacky stuff. Like if your cousin is ten years old and still thinks that stepping on cracks in the sidewalk is bad luck, well, that's a bit wacko.

But the *real* wackos are guys like King Nebuchad-nezzar, the ruler of the Babylonian Empire, who thought he was a cow. No kidding! King Neb became so proud that God made his mind blow a fuse. Next thing Neb knew, he was down on all fours chewing grass. What a sight! The king of Babylon out in the yard with the wild animals, sleeping in the dirt, his hair stringy and matted and his nails long and dirty (Daniel 4:32–33).

The word *wack* is something different. If a math test was particularly brutal, you'd say, "That test was wack." Or if you say, "That dude's wack," you're not saying he's crazy. You just mean he's not cool. (Okay, so maybe Nebuchadnezzar was both wacko *and* wack.)

FUN FACT

kook comes from the word cuckoo, which means crazy. Why does cuckoo mean crazy? Maybe because of those birds that come popping out of grandfather clocks, and all they say is "Cuckoo! Cuckoo!" over and over and over again.

Kooks and Cuckoos

A *kook* is a crazy person. Of course, sometimes it only *looks* like someone is a kook, when they're maybe not. Like when God told the prophet Isaiah to walk around naked for three years, and Isaiah *did* it (Isaiah 20:1–4). Lots of folks probably thought Isaiah had cracked. Not so. He was doing a skit to get people's attention. (Yep! He definitely did *that*!) Isaiah wanted to warn them that the Assyrian army was gonna conquer Egypt and march the prisoners off to Assyria—naked.

If people thought Isaiah was a kook, what did they think of the prophet Micah? Micah said, "I will go about barefoot and naked. I will howl like a jackal and moan like an owl" (Micah 1:8). He was not only running around naked, but he was howling and moaning. Well, Micah was doing a skit too—only this time it was the *Israelites* who would be marched off naked.

Nutty Nuts

When someone is a nut—or they're nuts or nutty—it means that they're crazy. (That's also why insane asylums are called nuthouses.) No telling how these expressions began, but there were lots of nuts in the Bible. For example, when Jacob sent his ten sons down to Egypt to buy some food, he sent some nuts with them. Wait, those nuts were pistachios and almonds (Genesis 43:11). Oh well.

Not everyone who does crazy-looking stuff actually *is* nuts, however. For example, God told the prophet Ezekiel to lie on the ground on his left side for 390 days, eating bread cooked over dried cow dung. And Zeke did it! Now, 390 days is a year and two months. That's a *long* time to lie on the ground chucking cow dung on the old campfire!

It seemed kind of nuts, but once again it was a skit. (Prophets were big into pantomimes back then.) Ezekiel's lie-down act was a warning that God would judge the Israelites, and they'd end up cooking food with cow manure (Ezekiel 4:4–15). Sure enough, they did.

Okay, before *you* try this, think things through: (1) Can you spare 390 days from school? (2) Can you really find that much cow dung? (3) Do you have a burning permit?

Lunatics

When people went crazy for a while and then returned to normal, folks used to think that this temporary insanity was caused by changes in the moon. (The Latin word for moon is *luna*.) That's why this illness was called *lunacy*, and crazy people were called *lunatics*. A full moon was supposed to be the worst time of all. People locked their doors whenever there was a full moon.

This superstition isn't true. If it were, the astronauts who landed on the moon would have gone completely crazy. They didn't. The Bible says, "The sun will not harm you by day, nor the moon by night" (Psalm 121:6).

Get Cooler

The story about David pretending to be insane is funny. However, if some guy is *actually* mentally ill, you shouldn't call him names or look down on him. Christians should have love and compassion for all people. If some kid's physically ill, you don't mock him, right? Same if he has a mental illness.

Avoid sticking labels on people who aren't mentally ill too. Of course, a lot of it's your motive and the tone of your voice. You can tell a friend, "You're nuts," and he jokes back, "You're the one who's mental." That's cool. And if some dude says something really *strange*, it's okay to blurt out, "You are out of your mind." That's what the Christians in Jerusalem said to Rhoda (Acts 12:15). The point is, try to avoid hurting others by what you say.

Practical Jokers

Clowning around can be fun. But some kids don't know when to pull the plug. They'll do anything for a laugh, even playing dangerous or scary tricks on others. The dictionary says a practical joke is "a trick having a victim." The Bible plants a STOP sign on that kind of humor. Proverbs 26:18–19 says: "Like a madman shooting firebrands or deadly arrows is a man who deceives his neighbor and says, 'I was only joking!'"

Teases and Twits

Twit comes from the old English word, *atwiten,* which meant "to tease or annoy." So people who twit are called twits. Generally it's *not* a good idea to tease people, but hey, sometimes it's necessary. Like when Elijah, God's prophet, was having a contest with the false prophets of Baal to see which god was the true God. The test: the real god had to send fire blazing down from heaven to burn up a sacrifice.

The pathetic prophets of Baal prayed all day long to Baal, but there was no answer, so Elijah taunted them, "Shout louder! Surely he is a god! Perhaps he is deep in thought, or busy, or traveling. Maybe he is sleeping and must be awakened!" (1 Kings 18:27). Elijah wasn't being so nice, but he did get a point across: Baal couldn't answer prayer because he didn't exist.

Oh, by the way, God *did* send down fire to burn up the sacrifice.

Jerks and Rude Dudes

A *jerk* goes beyond a twit. He's not just annoying. He's downright rude. Someone who jerks people around is a jerk. When the Jews were rebuilding the walls around Jerusalem, they hauled away tons of rubbish and lifted huge, heavy stones up into place. While they were sweating away, working hard, two of their enemies, Sanballat and Tobiah, walked up.

Sanballat ridiculed them, saying, "What are those feeble Jews doing? Will they restore their wall? ... Can they bring the stones back to life from those heaps of rubble?"

Tobiah joined in: "If even a fox climbed up on it, he would break down their wall of stones!" (Nehemiah 4:1–3).

These guys were genuine jerks. But you gotta remember Sanballat and Tobiah wanted to *kill* the Jews. You don't call some kid a jerk simply because he won't give you a stick of gum or he cuts in front of you in the food line.

Brats and Pests

Originally *brat* meant "a young animal." After a while, *brat* came to mean "bad children." These days, any kid who bothers others is called a brat or a pest. If he's really bad, he's called a *spoiled brat*.

A *bratwurst* does not mean worst brat, by the way. A bratwurst is a kind of sausage from Germany. This has absolutely nothing to do with the Bible, but we thought you'd want to know about it.

Creeps

A *creep* is someone who goes out of his way to be annoying and offensive. The worst example of that is Shimei (Shimmy-eye). One day Absalom pulled a surprise attack on King David, and David and his army had to flee. They were so broken up, they were crying as they left Jerusalem. Most Israelites were choked up too. As David went past, "the whole countryside wept aloud" (2 Samuel 15:23, 30).

One creep was not crying. A guy called Shimei "cursed as he came out. He pelted David and all the king's officials with stones." David's cousin wanted to kill Shimei, but David stopped him. Did Shimei clue in? No. He continued "cursing as he went and throwing stones at him and showering him with dirt" (2 Samuel 16:5–13).

Yikes! Creep or what?

Psychos

A psycho is *worse* than a creep. A *psycho* is a real whacko creep who has fun hurting other people for no reason. Sounds like King Saul. He had once been a good king, but Saul kept on disobeying God until one day God's Spirit left him and an evil spirit entered him. Then when David was sitting there playing Saul peaceful harp music, Saul grabbed his lance and tried to kill David. *Twice!* It's a good thing Saul wasn't a great aim (1 Samuel 16:14; 18:10–12).

Weirdo

A weirdo is someone who's *very* strange. King Saul makes such a good example, let's use him again. When he tried to kill David, David ran to the prophet Samuel's house. Saul chased him, but when he got there, God's Spirit totally overwhelmed him. Saul began prophesying. Okay, normal so far. Prophets did that kind of thing.

But what Saul did next was *not* normal: he ripped off all his clothes and lay on the ground naked all day and all night prophesying (1 Samuel 19:18–24). Now *that* is weird. Can't you just picture David getting up in the middle of the night, and there's Samuel sitting by the window?

David: "He still there?"

Samuel: "Yup. Naked and mumbling, facedown in the dirt."

Scoundrel

You probably have no idea what a scoundrel is, but since the Bible uses this slang term, it's high time you found out. A *scoundrel* is a tricky person with no morals, meaning he doesn't know right from wrong. The Bible says, "A scoundrel plots evil, and his speech is like a scorching fire" (Proverbs 16:27). Whoa! Give that guy some mouthwash!

The two sons of the high priest Eli were scoundrels. When Israelites came to sacrifice animals to the Lord, they had to cook the meat first, *then* the priests could take some. That was the law. But Eli's sons demanded their meat raw and threatened to fight the worshipers to get it. That would be like an usher wrestling you down in church and grabbing your piggy bank away from you.

Worse yet, these scoundrels forced themselves on the innocent women who served at the door of the tabernacle! *Yuck!* The Israelites were *sick* of Eli's sons and no one wanted to go to church any more (1 Samuel 2:12–24). No wonder God got rid of those guys.

Punks

The word *punk* has several meanings. First, it's talking about a practical joker. So if some kid dumps a bucket of water on you, you'd say, "Man! I got *punked*!" Second, it means a coward—especially a mouthy coward who likes to push people around. That's why you say you *got punked* if some kid bullies you.

A punk is also a kid with a bad attitude—he resents *any* kind of authority. He won't listen to his parents. He tunes out his teachers, and he even disrespects police. He's not afraid to trash-talk anyone, and his rebellious attitude often gets him in danger.

The youths that mocked the prophet Elisha were punks. Elisha was walking by, minding his own business—and part of his business was that he was bald—when a gang of bad eggs started mocking him, calling him Baldhead! Not smart. Elisha prayed, and two *very* mad bears came roaring out of the woods and mauled the punks (2 Kings 2:23–24). Warning: unless you are a bear and have a second bear with you as backup, don't mess with punks.

Bully

Bully means canned or pickled beef. Hmmm, that's probably not the meaning we're looking for. Another meaning for *bully* is a loud kid who picks on weaker kids. (By the way, *bully* comes from the Dutch word *boel*, which means friend.)

Goliath was a bully. (He wasn't a jar of pickled beef. He wasn't a friendly Dutchman.) Goliath was over nine feet tall and weighed about 850 pounds, so he thought it was great fun to dare the Israelites to fight him (1 Samuel 17:4–11). Of course we know the end of that story: David picked up a stone and used it to give Goliath a brain implant. (Ever wonder what that stone would sell for on eBay?)

Hotheads

Someone who loses his temper easily and gets into
fights is called a *hothead*. King Solomon said a guy
like that just doesn't learn. He's cruisin' for a bruisin'.
Rescue him out of trouble and you'll just have to rescue
him again later (Proverbs 19:19).

The men of Ephraim were hotheads. They got choked
over the stupidest ego stuff. A superwarrior named
Jephthah had just finished defeating Israel's enemies,
the Ammonites, and when the battle was over, the
men of Ephraim came running up, all ticked off. "Why
did you go to fight the Ammonites without calling us to
go with you?" they asked. "We're going to burn down
your house over your head."

Jephthah tried to talk some sense into them, but they
weren't listening. They got right in his face so he had to
fight them—and he won. Some 42,000 hotheads from
Ephraim died that day (Judges 12:1–6).

Insects

When a girl walks up to a guy, curls her lips and sneers,
"Insect!" she's saying, "You are an insignificant zero!
Oh, and by the way, I'm so much better than you!"
The apostle Paul had a different idea. Instead of calling
people worthless nothings, he said, "In humility con-
sider others better than yourselves" (Philippians 2:3).
Whoa! Radical idea, huh?

Of course, there's no helping people who consider *themselves* insects—like the ten Israelite spies who walked into Canaan, saw giants there, and came running back saying, "We seemed like grasshoppers in our own eyes, and we looked the same to them" (Numbers 13:33).

Sickos

Do *not* go calling anyone a *sicko* lightly, 'cause it's a strong term. But for the record, King Herod's family were all sickos. It started when Herod met Herodias, his brother's wife, and talked her into ditching her husband and marrying him. When Herodias moved into Herod's palace, her teenage daughter, Salome, tagged along. Next thing you know, Herod was drooling over Salome too. It gets sicker.

Now, Herodias *knew* what Herod was thinking, but she *used* it to manipulate Herod. You see, they had a prisoner in their dungeon—none other than John the Baptist. John had given Herod a tongue-lashing for marrying his brother's wife, so Herod locked John up. Herodias wanted to kill John, but Herod was afraid to hurt a righteous dude like John.

Then Herodias got her chance. Herod's birthday came along and he threw a huge banquet for his officials and officers. Herod and his guests were stuffing themselves and getting drunk as skunks when Herodias sent Salome in with *her* birthday present—a dance. Salome danced so appealingly that Herod sputtered, "Whatever you ask, I will give you ... up to half my kingdom."

Salome purred, "Give me here on a platter the head of John the Baptist." Herod nearly fell off his throne. But he'd promised, so he had someone clean the olives off the nearest platter and handed it to an executioner. A few minutes later the guy comes back with the gory gift. Can't you just see Salome smiling and wishing Herod a happy birthday as she carries it away?

Herod was sick, Herodias was sick, and Salome was sick. But poor John the Baptist ended up *dead* (Mark 6:14–28).

FUN FACTS

A grouch is a grumpy, mean person. This word comes from the old French word groucher, which means to murmur. Well, that fits! A grump is like a grouch. The word grump was invented when somebody mixed grunt and dump together. (What if they'd mixed them the other way and come up with drunt instead?) A crank is someone who is not only grouchy, but strange and hostile too. Funny though, 'cause if you say someone's cranky, you just mean they're in a bad mood.

Lowlifes

A *lowlife* is a person who does underhanded or disgusting stuff. If you call someone a *lowlife*, you're saying that they're a lower life form—subhuman. It's the same as calling someone an *animal* or an *insect*. Very few people fit this description. The Bible does talk about a few, however. It calls certain evil men "brute beasts, creatures of instinct, born only to be caught and destroyed" (2 Peter 2:12). Does anybody *you* know deserve to be called a lowlife? Probably not.

But it does fit some people—like King Manasseh of Judah. He became king when he was twelve, and this boy wonder went on a high-speed toboggan ride into evil. His dad loved God, but Manasseh built altars to false gods. This creep even practiced sorcery and was buddies with spiritualists and mediums.

Manasseh got so bad that when he became a dad, he sacrificed his own kid to the god Molech. He didn't stop there. "Manasseh also shed so much innocent blood that he filled Jerusalem from end to end" with dead bodies (2 Kings 21:16). God was *furious*.

You'd think there was no hope for a lowlife like that, right? You'd be surprised! God sent the Assyrian army against Judah. They captured Manasseh, stuck a hook in his nose, and made him walk all the way to Babylon, where he was chucked in prison. End of story? No. While this rotter rotted in prison, a miracle happened. He repented and prayed to God. Next thing you know, the Assyrians let Manny out of prison and he's sitting on his throne in Jerusalem again (without the nose hook).

Manasseh made good on his repentance. He chucked the pagan altars out of the temple, tore down the idols in the city, and threw them out the gates (2 Kings 21:1–18; 2 Chronicles 33:1–20).

A RECYCLED PSYCHO

Back a ways we told you that a psycho is a creep who enjoys hurting others. Well, a couple years after Jesus' resurrection, a psycho was terrorizing the city of Jerusalem. His name was Saul, and he was kicking in doors, arresting Christians—both men and women—and then dragging them off to prison to torture them. If they refused to curse Jesus' name, Saul had them killed. Christians grabbed their kids and ran from Jerusalem by the hundreds.

Then a miracle happened: Saul became a Christian himself! He changed his name to Paul and went around preaching the gospel. Paul knew how awful he had been before. He said, "Christ Jesus came into the world to save sinners—of whom I am the worst ... the worst of sinners" (Acts 8:1-3; 9:1-20; 26:9-11; 1 Timothy 1:15-16).

If there was hope for a psycho like Saul, there's hope for anyone.

GET DEEPER

That's the thing: often just when someone's bad enough to deserve the label creep or psycho, God gets hold of him, changes his heart, and turns him into a great guy. The lesson here is a simple one: you *cannot* once and for all write anyone off as a loser or a lost cause. Jesus can save *anyone*.

Sure, some kid may do dumb stuff, but that doesn't make him a permanent dummy. Someone may have blond moments, but that doesn't mean that person is an eternal ditz. A sibling may wuss out once or twice, but that doesn't make him or her a wuss now and forever. Your friend might be lazy now, but it doesn't mean he's stuck in lazy mode permanently.

Besides, even if someone *is* like that, you still gotta love him with God's love. Sure, you'll want to be praying for the dude to *change,* but in the meantime you gotta hold out hope.